Little Girls in Matching Dresses

and
Other Tales of Mothers,
Daughters & Grandmothers

COUNTRY LIVING

Little Girls
in
Matching
Dresses

AND

Other Tales of Mothers,
Daughters & Grandmothers

FAITH ANDREWS BEDFORD

HEARST BOOKS
A division of Sterling Publishing Co., Inc.

New York / London
www.sterlingpublishing.com

Copyright © 2009 by Hearst Communications, Inc.

Design by Alexandra Maldonado

Library of Congress Cataloging-in-Publication Data
Bedford, Faith Andrews.
Little girls in matching dresses : and other tales of mothers, daughters & grandmothers / Faith Andrews Bedford.
p. cm.
Includes index.
ISBN 978-1-58816-755-2
1. Bedford, Faith Andrews—Anecdotes. 2. Bedford, Faith Andrews—
Family—Anecdotes. 3. Family—United States—Anecdotes.
4. Country life—United States—Anecdotes. 5. Bedford family—Anecdotes.
6. Andrews family—Anecdotes. I. Title.
CT275.B5484A3 2009
973.92092—dc22
[B]
2008044995

10 9 8 7 6 5 4 3 2 1

Published by Hearst Books
A division of Sterling Publishing Co., Inc.
387 Park Avenue South, New York, NY 10016

Country Living and Hearst Books are trademarks of
Hearst Communications, Inc.

www.countryliving.com

For information about custom editions, special sales, premium
and corporate purchases, please contact Sterling Special Sales Department
at 800-805-5489 or specialsales@sterlingpublishing.com.

Distributed in Canada by Sterling Publishing
c/o Canadian Manda Group, 165 Dufferin Street
Toronto, Ontario, Canada M6K 3H6

Distributed in Australia by Capricorn Link (Australia) Pty. Ltd.
P.O. Box 704, Windsor, NSW 2756 Australia

Printed in USA

Sterling ISBN 978-1-58816-755-2

❧❧❧

It is to my sisters, Ellen and Beth,
who played such an important part in my life
and my stories, that I dedicate this book.
There are no better friends than sisters.
And there are no better sisters than you.

My deepest appreciation goes to
my husband Bob—friend, partner,
first editor, and chef
(when deadlines were looming).

table of contents

foreWord

Mother used to say that every day was Mother's Day. She did not like having a fuss made over something she loved doing—being a mother. But I know she was secretly pleased when we "surprised" her on Mother's day with breakfast in bed (scorched toast with marmalade and luke-warm coffee, the tray made festive with a sprig of lilac from her garden)." I don't need presents," she would often say, gathering us into her arms, "I have everything I need." Books, however, were the one exception. My sisters and I would pool our allowances for several weeks, then walk into the village to consult with Mrs. McFeatters who owned the corner bookshop. Like any good bookseller, she knew all her customers and their tastes. Over the years, she guided us to slim volumes of poetry, a number of classics, and books that I later loved as much as Mother did.

Mother loved to read to us. Some of my earliest memories are of sitting in her lap, turning the pages as she read *Winnie-the-Pooh*. Being a bookworm runs in the family; it's an inherited trait. My grandparents read me the stories they used to read to my parents. Rainy days meant long hours snuggled with them on the sofa as they "did all the voices" of the characters in such classics as *Little Women* and *The Adventures of Tom Sawyer*, *Charlotte's Web* and *Treasure Island*. Those books eventually ended up on the "children's shelf"—the lowest shelf of our family bookcase. When my little sisters, and later my children, asked me to read to them that's where I found the books we all loved.

Mother treasured the simple, quiet things in life, the ordinary, the daily: braiding our hair in the morning before school, showing us the difference between a weed and a flower, hanging sheets on the line so they would "smell like sunshine," helping us carefully fill the bird feeder then teaching us the names of all our feathered visitors.

These memories recall for me Mother's pleasures in the dailyness of life. They were little things, really, but things that acknowledged her joy in our curiosity and creativity, things that spoke of caring and encouragement.

As I began to write the stories that appeared in my "Kids in the Country" column in *Country Living* magazine, I reached back into those wonderful growing-up years for inspiration. Mother loved reading my reminiscences of our matching "sister dresses," learning the art of writing thank you notes, hiding behind my Father's red leather chair so she wouldn't make me put down my book and go play outside ("So that's where you were," she laughed). My story of how she taught us to hunt for sea glass at the edge of the waves took her back to her own sunlit moments by the seashore.

As a parent, amidst the joyous chaos of raising three children, I found myself swept along in the hectic cycle of driving to lessons and sports, activities and errands. Sometimes it was a delicate balance trying to juggle work, family, chores, marriage and, especially, quiet time to appreciate everyone and everything. The busy-ness of life sometimes overwhelmed the appreciation of the daily-ness. Reflecting on the gifts that my mother and grandmothers gave me, I recall their enjoyment of and commitment to simple, empty time: time to savor life's little rituals, time for spontaneous adventures and discoveries, moments for quiet enjoyment of each other, time to just appreciate the ordinary.

Many of the traditions Mother began, I've continued. And, as our children have grown, we've added new ones. Creating stories for and about my family is one of those. As I write, I am transported to a place where I can, once again, see the world through the eyes of a child. I remember the sense of wonder at the new, the comfort in the familiar as well as the closeness of family.

As a child, I gave my Mother gifts of books for her special day. Now I write them. But they are still and will always be my gift to her.

time and a bottle

A dozen pieces of sea glass march across the windowsill above my kitchen sink. They look like small sugar candies. One is pale green, and several are beige or brown. There are quite a few clear pieces; two are the color of lapis lazuli.

Once, these shards were hard and sharp—a danger to barefoot beachcombers. Perhaps some came from a jar thrown overboard by a careless boater. Others could be remnants of a bottle left lying in the sand after a picnic. Now, after years of tumbling about in the surf, the glass has mellowed, their colors faded—merely pretty reminders of a once-sharp brilliance.

As children, my sisters and I combed the beach for these bits of frosted color. Shells were everywhere, but sea glass was a treasure to be pounced upon eagerly. Our eyes became highly trained as we walked slowly near the water's edge, probing the drifts of small rocks and shells that the tides rearranged each day.

"There's one," Ellen would shout as she glimpsed a bit of green amidst the white shells.

"Oooohh, blue!" Beth would gasp when she spied that rarest of colors.

Sometimes the glass was still transparent and slightly sharp. It had not achieved perfect smoothness.

"Not done yet," we would declare if we found such a piece. "Throw it back."

And so we would fling the bit of glass as far out into the sea as our small arms were able, hoping that we might come again next summer and find it finished, worthy of adding to our collection.

Mother told us that long ago, in some fishing villages, people used to simply throw their trash into the harbor. From those watery middens, the fingers of the tide coaxed bits and pieces of glass and deposited them along the seacoast.

"Could our sea glass have come from anywhere?" we asked her.

She nodded. "And some of it might be quite old."

Mother had once told us that France lay on the other side of the ocean from where we made sandcastles on our broad stretch of beach. I looked out across the water and

imagined that the misty white bit of glass in my hand had come from a perfume bottle thrown into the water a century ago by an elegant lady in Paris.

As children, my sisters and I combed the beach for these bits of frosted color. Shells were everywhere, but sea glass was a treasure to be pounced upon eagerly.

Sea glass comes in many different hues and colors. Green can range from bright chartreuse to dark gray-green—the color the sky sometimes takes on just before a storm. My sisters and I reasoned that these green bits must have come from ginger ale or maybe even French wine bottles. Pale aquamarine, we assumed, came from Coke bottles, and the brown bits, we were sure, came from our favorite soda pop—Orange Crush. But sea glass of pale amethyst and pink were mysteries. The rarest find of all was a piece of deep cobalt-blue sea glass. Such a treasure was easy to spot, for nothing in nature, not a shell, nor a rock, nor a bit of seaweed, possessed that astonishing sapphire color.

In the past, every time I went for a walk on a beach, I always found a piece of sea glass, sometimes several. This summer, for the first time in my life, I came back empty-handed. The environmentalist in me was pleased to see that people are no longer so careless with glass. The child in me was bitterly disappointed.

When my own children were small, I taught them the art of hunting for sea glass. "You need to walk slowly," I said holding their hands in mine. "Sweep your eyes back and forth across the drifts of shells and pebbles and, pretty soon, you will be able to spot the sea glass quickly."

But the children would race ahead of me. And I would laugh, realizing that asking a child to walk slowly is like trying to hold back an incoming tide.

And yet, they often did find the sea glass we so carefully sought. In time, they became expert beachcombers.

Over the years, we've collected jars full of the lovely stuff. My husband once made me a wind chime by hang-

This summer, for the first time in my life, I came back empty-handed. The environmentalist in me was pleased to see that people are no longer so careless with glass. The child in me was bitterly disappointed.

ing several shards of sea glass from a piece of driftwood. When we suspended it from a tree, it made a sound like the tinkling of ice cubes in a glass of cold lemonade.

But the pieces on my windowsill are the best of the best. One of my favorites is a piece of deep red glass frosted to a soft raspberry color. Another piece has been shaped by nature into a perfect pale green heart. And there are several tiny azure bits of sea glass, just the color of an August-blue sky.

How long does it take the ocean to turn a broken bottle into sea glass? A month? A few years? Decades?

Perhaps as long as it takes for a child to master the art of walking slowly. As I remember myself and my sisters racing down the beach in our hunt for the precious frosted glass, I see the three of us, our long braids flying out behind us. The waves whisper on the shore, tickling our toes; we laugh in delight as we try to avoid their reach. There is my mother standing tall, her hand shading her eyes against the brilliant sun as she watches us whirl about on the sand. Our bright bathing suits (green for me, red for Beth, blue for Ellen) help her distinguish us, one from the other. The demure skirt of her own suit ruffles gently in the warm sea breeze, and the gulls soar high above.

The currents of life have carried me far from those days. As I've tumbled about through the years, my own rough edges have, hopefully, grown smoother, too. The blond pigtails are gone. As Nature frosts sea glass, so has she frosted my hair.

I rearrange the bits of glass on the windowsill and realize that I do not mourn the sharp glitter of youth. My life has acquired a certain soft patina. I've mellowed. Years of watching nature have brought an awareness of the constancy of change. I have gained an appreciation of the need to be flexible, having seen the fragility of things that are not.

I pick up a piece of creamy yellow glass, triangular in shape, and hold it in the hollow of my hand. I remember when I found this one. My sisters and I had never seen such a color. "Is it finished yet?" asked Beth. "Or does it need more time? Shall we throw it back?"

"No," I answered, putting it in my bucket. "It's perfect."

Years of watching **nature** have brought an awareness of the constancy of change. I have gained an **appreciation** of the need to be flexible, having seen the **fragility** of things that are not.

sister dresses

My sister's car disappeared over the top of the hill, her faint "toot" of farewell telling me she had turned onto the main road. The dust settled on our lane as I turned to the pile of boxes she left behind.

When Mother died, Dad gave up the summerhouse.

"Come and take what you want, girls," he had said to us, and so we did.

I chose the tall secretary desk where Mother sat so often writing letters by a sunny window. Beth chose a painting of the summer house itself. Ellen picked a statue of horses, for she and Mother had shared a love of riding. After the moving van left with the things that Dad wanted, my sisters and I had lingered in the cottage going through drawers full of old letters, boxes of slides, albums of faded photos—the collective memory of a family. We had put it all into a dozen boxes, then each of us chose four. Beth dropped off my boxes first; Ellen's house was her next stop.

I sat down on the top step of the porch and opened a box marked "Albums." There were photographs of my father, resplendent in his naval uniform, and one of my mother leaning against their first car. Farther on was a faded picture of the family gathered for my christening, the women elegant in hats and gloves, the men's faces shadowed by their fedoras. As I slowly leaf through the pages, the family grows, we buy our first house, the cars get bigger. Then, there on the last page, is the picture of us in our sister dresses.

I could almost feel the starched ruffles and hear the rustle of the crinolines that were needed to keep the skirts nice and full. How well I remember Mother's delight when she found these dresses at the children's shop in the village. There was one in my size and one for Ellen but no size four for Beth. We were so excited when Mrs. Page, the shopkeeper, told us she felt sure she could order one for Beth that would come in time for Easter.

When the big box arrived in early April, we gathered around Mother while she lifted the dresses out, one by one. The pink tissue paper rustled as she held each one up. They were made of clouds of dotted Swiss—white organdy with blue, flocked dots. The skirt and collar were trimmed with tiny blue bows.

"To match your eyes," Mother had said.

We were allowed to try them on just once so that we could have a "fashion show" for Dad that evening. As we twirled into the dining room in our new finery, he burst into applause. Ellen and I daintily grasped the ruffled skirts and executed our best curtsies; Beth scrunched her dress up in her chubby little hands and made a close approximation of a bow, almost toppling over in the process. Then we had to carefully hang them up until Easter.

As I looked at the photograph, I could almost feel the pale April sunshine on our faces. We undoubtedly resisted putting on coats to go to church. They surely would have crushed those beautiful dresses and besides, then how could anyone see how wonderfully we matched?

In time, I handed my dress down to Ellen and she handed hers down to Beth. Finally, only Beth had one of those beautiful dresses, its bow a bit bedraggled after countless wearings by three little girls. But those dotted Swiss dresses were only the beginning of a long parade of matching sister outfits. Mother obviously was so pleased with the effect that she began an Easter tradition. I remember the year of the blue calicos and the year we all had matching yellow jumpers. Even Dad got into the spirit of things when he came back from a business trip to Arizona with Mexican dresses for each of his girls—even one for Mother.

Gradually, as we grew older, I think Mother saw how very different we all were becoming and just stopped buying us matching dresses.

Those wonderful white dresses, with rows and rows of bright ribbons edging the wide collars and hems, had skirts that were cut in a complete circle. Dad put Ravel's Bolero on the record player and we spun madly about the living room, our beribboned skirts fluttering like crazed butter-flies. At last, we crashed, giggling, into a heap. Dad, quite pleased with our reaction to his gift, sat in his armchair and grinned his "that's-my-girls" smile.

As I looked at the photograph, I remembered those very first sister dresses so clearly that I am somewhat sur-prised that I cannot remember the last ones. Maybe Mother knew we were outgrowing the idea. Perhaps it was I who, at the sophisticated age of fourteen, first protested, saying something like "Really Mother, I'm much too old for that sort of thing."

Gradually, as we grew older, I think Mother saw how very different we all were becoming and just stopped buying us matching dresses.

By the time we were in our twenties, our lives were on three very distinct tracks. Our wardrobes clearly reflected our different worlds. I carried babies on my back; my clothes tended toward blue jeans and sweatshirts. Ellen was putting together outfits that could have been in the pages of Vogue. And Beth, a potter who actually went to the original Woodstock, favored bell-bottoms and Indian blouses.

I smile now to think of the sight we must have made: Three grown women, dressed in red-flannel nighties, whirling madly through a jumble of empty boxes and wrapping paper.

Mother would shake her head in bemused bewilderment and say to Dad, "How did we get three such different daughters?" He would merely smile in response.

Though our lives have continued along different pathways, the circle draws closer as we grow older and once again realize how similar we are. Now we are all mothers and equally challenged by our various roles. Although our wardrobes are still very different, we all seem to be moving toward variations on "classic." Last Christmas, I gave all the women in the family silk blouses. Same style, different colors. Everyone loved them.

Mother didn't realize what a tradition she started. When my own daughters were little, I often made them sister dresses. When I was expecting my third child, I made myself a maternity dress out of some bright pink cotton. Eleanor, my older daughter, loved the fabric, so I made a jumper for her out of the scraps. That baby turned out to be a girl. So, in a way, my daughters' sister dresses started even before birth.

For as long as I can remember, Dad had always given Mother a beautiful nightgown each Christmas. They were long and silky, with plenty of lace. When we were little, we loved to stroke their satiny smoothness. With Mother gone, that tradition would stop. The first Christmas without her was bittersweet. The tree sparkled, but there was no big, pink box from "Sweet Dreams" beneath it.

We put on happy faces for the sake of our children, but all the little touches that Mother always added to Christmas were missing. Suddenly, Ellen drew out from behind the tree three identical white boxes. On the lids, written in Dad's bold hand, were the words "From the

Nightie Gnome." We opened them and lifted out three identical red-flannel nightshirts.

We whooped with delight as we pulled them out of the tissue paper, then ran down the hall to put them on. When we came back into the living room to show off our sister nighties, Dad had put Ravel's Bolero on the stereo. We joined hands and did an impromptu dance. As the music grew louder, we twirled around faster and faster, ignoring the wide eyes of our disbelieving husbands and the gaping mouths of our children.

I smile now to think of the sight we must have made: Three grown women, dressed in red-flannel nighties, whirling madly through a jumble of empty boxes and wrapping paper. When the music ended in a clash of cymbals, we crashed, giggling, into a heap.

Our husbands shook their heads in wonder. The younger children nearly keeled over with embarrassment while the older ones held their sides with laughter. Dad just cracked his "that's-my-girls" grin.

thank you, uncle arthur

One of the nice things about having grown children is that I don't have to bug them about writing thank-you notes anymore.

When my three children were little, I voiced their gratitude for the gifts they received in a family letter. By the time they were three, they could draw a picture of their present and dictate a thank-you note that I would include with the drawing. But once they were in school, they wrote their own thank-yous—with much prodding.

In the days following Christmas, I would frequently ask, "Have you written to thank Grandy for the book yet?" or "What did you say to Aunt Dorothy about that sweater?"

I would be met with mumbles and shrugs, clear indications that the note had not been written. I grew weary of nagging. The children grew increasingly mother-deaf. It would have been easier to write the notes myself, I often thought.

One Christmas, overwhelmed by frustration, I declared that no one would be allowed to read a new book, play with a new toy, or wear a new outfit until the thank-you note for it had been mailed. But still the children procrastinated and grumbled.

"It takes too long," groaned Eleanor.

Something snapped.

"OK," I said. "Everyone, into the car."

One Christmas, overwhelmed by frustration, I declared that no one would be allowed to read a new book, play with a new toy, or wear a new outfit until the thank-you note for it had been mailed.

"Where are we going?" Sarah asked in bewilderment.

"To buy a Christmas present," I said tersely.

"But it's after Christmas," she protested, putting on her coat.

"No arguing," I said, in a tone of voice that the children knew meant exactly that.

As the children piled into the car, I told them, "You're going to see just how much time those who care about you spend when they give you a present."

"We know," grumbled Drew, slumped in the back seat.

"You don't know," I said, handing him a pad of paper and a pencil. "Please mark down the time we left home."

When we reached the village, Drew noted our arrival time. The girls helped me select birthday presents for my sisters at the Smart Shoppe. Then we turned around and drove home.

Bursting free from the confines of the car, the children headed for the sleds they'd left at the top of the hill. "Not so fast," I said. "We are not finished yet."

"But we bought the presents," Eleanor said, her hands on her hips.

"We've got to wrap them," I said, beckoning the children inside. They slouched through the door and waited while I got out the gift-wrap box.

"Drew," I asked. "Did you jot down the time we got home?" He held up the pad and nodded. "OK, please time the girls while they wrap the presents."

I made the children some cocoa while they wrapped Ellen and Beth's scarves. Drew cut the ribbon and timed his sisters.

After they had finished tying up the bows, they looked at me expectantly. "Now what?" asked Sarah.

"How long did this all take?" I asked Drew.

He considered his notes and said, "It took us twenty-eight minutes to get to town and fifteen minutes to buy the presents. Then it was thiry-eight minutes to get back home 'cause we had to buy gas."

"And how long did it take us to wrap the boxes?" Eleanor asked.

"Each of you did one present in two minutes," Drew said, looking at his watch.

"And how many minutes will it take us to go back into town and mail these presents?" I asked.

"Fifty-six minutes, round trip," Drew figured. "If we don't need gas."

"But you forgot standing-in-line time," said Sarah, who had often been the one to help me mail our packages.

"Yes," I agreed. "And, at Christmas, that can be a long time." Our post office can only hold about ten people. Twelve, if two or three are children. Between Thanksgiving and Christmas, those at the end of the line might shiver outside in the cold.

"Okay," Drew said, refiguring his sum. "We probably need to add about fifteen minutes for mailing."

"So," I said, "what's the total time we would spend to give someone a present?"

Drew added up his figures. "Two hours and twenty-eight minutes," he answered, tapping his pencil on the pad.

I laid a piece of stationery, an envelope, and a pen beside everyone's cocoa cup.

"Now," I said. "Please write a thank-you note and be sure to mention the present by name and tell what fun you will have using it."

The children rolled their eyes. Silence reigned as they gathered their thoughts; soft pen scratchings and cocoa sipping followed.

"Done," said Eleanor licking her envelope and pressing it closed.

"Me too," echoed Sarah handing me her note.

"That took us three minutes," Drew said, sealing his letter.

"Is three minutes really too much to ask of you to thank someone for a thoughtful gift that may have taken them two and a half hours to choose and send to you?" I asked.

The children looked down at the table and shook their heads.

"It's a good idea to get in the habit now," I said. "In time you'll want to write thank-you notes for many things."

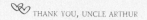

Drew groaned, "Like for what?"

"Like for dinners or lunches," I said. "Or weekends at someone's home, or the time someone takes to give you advice or help on college applications or careers."

"Careers?!" Drew gasped; his first career as the family lawn-mowing man was currently on seasonal hold.

"So," Eleanor asked, "what happens if you don't write someone a thank-you?"

"Practically speaking, they'll never know if the present arrived," I said. "But mostly, they might decide that you are thoughtless and ungrateful."

"And rude?" Eleanor added.

"And rude," I agreed. I looked at the children seriously. "And if you don't have three minutes to spend on them, they might decide they don't have time to spend on you."

Sarah thought for a minute and said, "And you won't get any more presents!" Her eyes grew wide with horror at the thought.

"Did you have to write thank-yous when you were a kid?" Drew asked.

"Absolutely."

"What did you say?" he asked. I could tell he was formulating the rest of his notes.

"I really don't recall," I answered. "It was a long time ago."

Then I remembered Uncle Arthur.

Uncle Arthur was my great-grandfather's youngest brother. I had never met him, yet every year he sent me a Christmas gift. He was blind and lived next door to his

Uncle Arthur was my great-grandfather's youngest brother. I had never met him, yet every year he sent me a Christmas gift.

niece, Becca. Each Christmas, she sat down with him and wrote out a five-dollar check to each of his dozens of great- and great-great nieces and nephews. I always wrote and told him how I had spent the money.

When I went to school in New England, I finally had the chance to visit Uncle Arthur in his old house near Salem's harbor. I was fascinated by his ability to find his way around his warren of little rooms. Some had ceilings so low that he came close to bumping his head. He fixed us tea and, as we chatted, he told me that he had always enjoyed my notes.

"You remember them?" I asked in surprise. "You must get so many."

"Yes," he replied. "But I've saved some of my favorites."

He waved toward a highboy by the window. "Would you get the packet of letters out of the top drawer?" he asked. "It's wrapped in ribbon."

I found the letters and brought them to him. He laughed. "Could you find yours and read it to me, please? I can't, you know."

I had almost forgotten his blindness and was glad he could not see my crimson face.

I quickly found my handwriting on one of the faded envelopes. Taking out the old letter, I read: "Dear Uncle Arthur, I am writing this to you as I sit under the hair dryer at the beauty salon. Tonight is the Holiday Ball at the high school, and I am spending your Christmas check having my hair done for the party. Thank you so very much. I know I'll have a wonderful time, in part because of your thoughtful gift. Love, Faith."

"Dear Uncle Arthur... Tonight is the Holiday Ball at the high school, and I am spending your Christmas check having my hair done for the party. Thank you so very much. I know I'll have a wonderful time...

"And did you?" asked Uncle Arthur.

"Have a good time?" I asked.

He nodded.

I thought back to that wonderful evening so many years ago. "Definitely," I replied with a smile I wished he could see.

Sarah's tug at my sleeve pulled me back to the present. "What are you smiling at?" she asked.

I told the children about Uncle Arthur's gifts and my surprise and pleasure that he had kept my note. I told them I was glad I had written a note each year; they obviously meant a lot to him.

"And did you look beautiful?" asked Sarah.

"My date said he thought I did," I laughed.

"Who did you go to the ball with? What did you wear?" asked Eleanor, no doubt visions of Cinderella filling her head.

"I think I have a picture of that evening," I said, going over to the bookshelves and pulling down a rather battered scrapbook. I opened it to a picture of me standing in front of my parents' fireplace. I'm wearing a strapless, black-velvet evening dress, and my hair is arranged in an elaborate French twist held firm with plenty of hairspray. Beside me, a handsome young man beams as he hands me a corsage.

… my hair is arranged in an elaborate French twist held firm with plenty of hairspray. Beside me, a handsome young man beams as he hands me a corsage. "But that's Daddy!" Eleanor exclaimed, looking at the picture with surprise.

"But that's Daddy!" Eleanor exclaimed, looking at the picture with surprise.

I nodded and smiled. "You looked pretty," Sarah said.

"Thank you," I replied. "That's what Daddy said."

As the children settled down to finish the rest of their notes, I stroked the faded petals of the dried gardenia pasted next to the photograph.

This past Christmas, Bob and I celebrated our fortieth anniversary. Thank you, Uncle Arthur.

the jewelry box

Tonight is our anniversary and my husband is taking me out. I look through my closet and pick out a deep green velvet dress with long sleeves and a high neck. It looks wonderful with my mother's seed pearl neck-lace and my grandmother's tiny pearl earrings.

As I sit at my dressing table, my daughter, Eleanor, perches beside me. She loves to watch me get dressed for special occasions.

"Mama," she addresses my reflection in the mirror, "May I pick out your jewelry?"

" Of course," I reply. She opens the drawer where I keep my jewelry box and begins to sift through the contents. There are the macaroni necklaces she made me in kinder-garten and the locket my husband gave me when we were

As I come down the stairs, my beads swinging and the brass earrings flashing in the light, I look down and see Eleanor's proud face. "You look beautiful," she sighs.

engaged. In a little box Eleanor finds my old Girl Scout pin and some badges.

She holds several pairs of earrings up to her small ears, then discards them. She tries on several necklaces and shakes her head. At last, with a little cry of delight, she pounces on a pair of long, dangly earrings from Ceylon. They are set with flashing mirrors, obviously left over from the seventies. I wore them with bell bottoms and tunics. In another box she finds two long ropes of beads from the same era.

She drapes the beads around my neck and hands me the earrings. I put them on and give my head a little shake. The earrings glitter brightly.

'Perfect!" She sighs with pleasure. We grin at each other in the mirror

As Eleanor races out of the room to tell her father that I am almost ready, I remember how, when I was Eleanor's age, I used to watch, entranced, as my own Mother prepared for an evening out.

While she pinned up her French twist, I would ask her to tell me where each piece had come from.

In a velvet case lay a beautiful garnet necklace and matching earrings. Mother told me that they belonged to her grandmother who wore them to Boston, where she had seen the famous Sarah Bernhardt perform.

The seed pearl necklace had been given to Mother by her godmother as a wedding present. Like me, she always wore it with the tiny pearl earrings her grandmother left her. Now I have inherited both.

My favorite things in the drawer were the gifts my Father had given her. In a velvet box was a necklace of rhinestones that glittered with the brilliance of real diamonds. Mother told me they were not diamonds at all, but I thought she looked just like a princess.

When Father went on a business trip to Arizona, he brought Mother back a ring with a big square piece of turquoise. It just fit her ring finger; it was too big for my thumb.

For her fortieth birthday, he presented her with some earrings from India. The black enamel had been cut away to reveal silver figures of dancing women bent into impossible positions My sisters and I tried to imitate them. We couldn't.

The Christmas I was ten I had saved up enough money to buy Mother some earrings at the five and dime: two red plastic bells hung from tiny bows The edges had been sprinkled with silver glitter Mother wore them all Christmas day. She shook her head frequently to show us how they actually made a little tinkling sound.

A few days later, I came into her room just in time to help zip up her black and white taffeta evening dress.

"Will you pick out some earrings for me, dear?" she asked.

Opening her drawer I sorted through the options. Her dress was pretty, I thought, but it needed a bit of color. I proudly pulled out the little red plastic bells.

"Just the thing!' she said, putting them on. I looked at her and thought no one ever was more beautiful.

My husband's voice pulls me back to the present. 'Ready?" he asks.

"Almost," I reply, putting Mother's pearls and Grandmother's earrings back into my jewelry box.

As I come down the stairs, my beads swinging and the brass earrings flashing in the light, I look down and see Eleanor's proud face. "You look beautiful," she sighs.

"Only with your help." I reply as I kiss her good night. She will be asleep by the time I return.

the honor jar

The produce stand down at the crossroads has added "Silver Queen Corn" to the long list of fruits and vegetables for sale. That's always a sure sign that it's the peak of harvest season. As I wave to the farmer, I remember the year we always refer to as the "summer of the bumper crops."

Ample rain and mild weather kept the lettuce from bolting early and the tomatoes from scorching. For some reason, the squash beetles didn't appear, and the potato bugs fled from my hot-pepper spray, just as they were supposed to.

We had fresh vegetables at every meal, including breakfast. Zucchini was served fried, baked, stuffed, and hidden in meat loaf. Corn on the cob and sliced tomatoes, always family favorites, began to be met with groans.

I used up all my canning jars, the freezer was full to bursting, and the porch rafters were festooned with strings of sliced squash hanging to dry in the summer breeze. One evening, I sank wearily down at the dinner table and said, "The garden is overflowing."

"I suppose you've put up as much as you can," my husband said.

I smiled weakly and nodded.

"You could give some to the neighbors," he offered helpfully.

"I've done that," I sighed. "Caroline and Ruth almost hide now when they see me coming."

The children, who had been listening silently while gamely downing yet another meal of beans, began whispering among themselves.

Piled high with multicolored vegetables, the Red Flyer looked like a festive gypsy wagon. ... The combination of freshly scrubbed vegetables and three eager, expectant faces must have been irresistible. They sold out by ten o'clock.

"How about if we have a produce stand?" Drew asked.

"That's a good idea, dear," I said. "But I really don't have time to set one up."

"We'll do it," Drew offered.

"All by ourselves," Eleanor added.

I must have looked skeptical, for Sarah piped up, "That way you'll have much less to pick, Mom."

I laughed and looked at Bob. He grinned at the kids. "OK. It's all yours."

The next morning the children were out in the garden even before the morning mists had lifted. By eight, they'd turned my kitchen into a small battle station.

The girls polished tomatoes to a ruby glow while Drew carefully arranged zucchinis in an old enamel bowl. In the basement, Sarah found some green plastic berry baskets I'd been saving for a Christmas project. She filled them with exactly thirty green beans each. Finally satisfied, they loaded their harvest into Eleanor's wagon. Piled high with multicolored vegetables, the Red Flyer looked like a festive gypsy wagon.

To the mailbox, they tacked a brown paper bag on which Eleanor had written in bold letters, "Fresh Produce." Then, they sat down on a blanket in the shade of the big maples and waited for their first customer.

The combination of freshly scrubbed vegetables and three eager, expectant faces must have been irresistible. They sold out by ten o'clock.

As they spread the change out on the kitchen table, they enthusiastically plotted the next day's stand.

"Let's sell flowers, too," suggested Sarah, always my helper when it came to flower arrangements.

"Can we grub for some new potatoes, Mom?" Eleanor asked.

"As long as you leave the deep ones for the fall digging, sure."

By ten the next morning, the air was hot and sultry, and the wagon was still half full. At noon the kids came trudging up the lane with a few boxes of beans left.

"Looks like green beans for dinner tonight," I said. Sarah rolled her eyes and made a face.

At dinner they reported, "We sold almost everything, but lots of cars passed us by."

"Maybe you need a bigger stand to attract more attention," Bob said.

"Would that take money?" Eleanor asked looking concerned.

Bob laughed, "I've probably got enough scrap lumber in the barn."

That Saturday was filled with the sounds of hammering and sawing. By evening, the children's faces and hands were so covered with paint spatters that I felt as though I was serving dinner to a tribe of warriors. Bob confessed to amazement at how three children could use up twelve years of accumulated paint in just two hours. The new stand was painted white; the girls had decorated it with multicolored vines and flowers. A large sign proclaimed Fresh-Picked Produce. It took all of us to carry the finished product down to the mailbox.

"I don't think there's enough money here." He looked at me in dismay. ... My heart ached as I looked at the three sad little faces.

On Monday, Sarah's jelly jars of fresh flowers nodded gaily in the morning breeze. Eleanor had piled scrubbed mounds of new potatoes on paper plates. Customers stopped by regularly. But the fun of making change in the noonday sun began to pale. Although the children enjoyed dropping the little piles of change into their piggy banks, they grew weary of turning down invitations to go swimming or bike riding.

"Minding the store" was quickly losing its appeal.

"How about using the honor system?" Bob asked one evening.

Three puzzled faces turned to him.

"You see that often at country stands," he explained. "Just list the prices and put out a jar for people to put their money in."

The children looked doubtful but decided to give it a try. Eleanor carefully made a price list. Drew cut a slit in the top of an old jar and Sarah lettered a sign: Honor Jar. Make Your Own Change.

The next day they set up their stand, then returned to the cool of the house and waited. Drew couldn't resist checking the stand at lunchtime. He returned to the house, his face jubilant.

"Half the vegetables are gone and the jar's almost full of money."

By evening only three tomatoes were left. Ever the realist, Drew had made a list of what they put out and what the profit should be. Allowing for the unsold tomatoes, it came out perfectly. Actually, ten cents over.

Excited by the idea of a produce stand that tended itself, the children faithfully harvested the garden each morning and filled the wooden shelves with our bumper crops.

But a week later, as Drew was tallying up the change in the jar, he paused. "I don't think there's enough money here." He looked at me in dismay.

Eleanor and Sarah quickly helped count the pile of change again. Drew checked his list and totaled up what should have been in the jar once more.

"We're $2.40 short," he groaned.

Silence filled the kitchen. My heart ached as I looked at the three sad little faces.

"Maybe some poor people needed food and just didn't have any money," Eleanor said.

"We'll keep the jar out," Drew said firmly. "Maybe I made a mistake."

For three days, the vegetables sold and the money in the jar came out even. But the next evening, Drew and the girls came into the kitchen looking downcast.

"We added it all up, Mom, and someone is taking vegetables again."

I made a small sign. …She read, "If you need vegetables but cannot pay, please help yourself. Or pay later. And may things get better for you soon."

I sat down at the table with the children.

"Eleanor was right. Someone probably needed food and just didn't have the money. At least not now."

"It's not like we don't have more than we need for ourselves anyway," Sarah added.

I smiled at her and took a blank card from my recipe box. I made a small sign.

"Would you like to put this by the Honor Jar tomorrow?" I said, handing it to Eleanor.

She read, "If you need vegetables but cannot pay, please help yourself. Or pay later. And may things get better for you soon."

"Would you like to add your signatures at the bottom?" I asked.

The children looked at each other. One by one they signed their names.

In the weeks following, sometimes the Honor Jar was a bit short. But sometimes the change in the jar equaled more than the value of the day's vegetables. At the end of the summer, according to Drew's careful calculations, it had all evened out.

a light in the window

Moving day was drawing to a close. The van rumbled down the lane, leaving us with three hungry children, a frightened cat, and a mountain of boxes to unpack. Our new home seemed vacant and lonely; the nearest neighbor was about a mile down the road. I could see a faint light glimmering through the woods.

Presently, I heard the crunch of tires on gravel; a small pickup truck pulled in beside the barn. When I opened the door, I was greeted by a warm smile. Our new neighbor, Marian, had brought us dinner, friendship, and advice.

My little red address book, full of all the names and numbers a family needs to function, was of no use in this new place. I peppered Marian with questions. Who was a

good vet? Where could I find aged manure for the garden? Was there a good plumber in town?

I learned with dismay that the nearest dentist was thirty miles away, but Marian assured me that the drive was beautiful.

She was right. As we drove down the valley, the hills were ablaze with autumn colors. Sugar maples bordered the old stone walls, and yellow willows hung over the stream that meandered alongside the road. In the golden meadows, cows contentedly grazed. We all decided that our favorites were the belted Galloways, whose wide band of white in the middle of their black bodies made us think of Oreo cookies.

We saw that four or five houses on the left side of the road and three on the right all had a single candle lit. I asked Marian if she knew why, and she answered, "It's the way it's always been."

By the time we left Dr. Thomasson's office, dusk was beginning to settle. As we passed the edge of town, Drew asked, "Why does each house have a Christmas candle in the window when it isn't even Halloween?"

I remembered that the Snydersville Apple Festival was slated for the coming weekend; we planned to help with the cider pressing. Perhaps this was some sort of tradition, part of the festivities.

That evening, when I called the cat in, she did not come. Kate had been confused ever since the move, meowing forlornly as she wandered through the unfamiliar house. The following morning, she was still missing.

Then winter closed in. The children worried about Kate, and I tried to reassure them that she had probably found a nice warm barn to stay in for the winter. She was hibernating, I said, like a bear.

Mud season delayed the plowing. Spring chores piled up. Finally, one warm March afternoon as the first daffodils were blooming, the children and I headed back to Snydersville to buy new shoes. Sarah couldn't decide between the red sneakers or the white, and Eleanor took a long time finding just the right pair of party shoes. It was growing late by the time we left for home. Dusk was beginning to fall.

"Look," said Eleanor as we neared the outskirts of the village, "those houses still have lights in the window."

We saw that four or five houses on the left side of the road and three on the right all had a single candle lit.

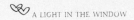

I asked Marian if she knew why, and she answered, "It's the way it's always been." Then she laughed. "That's a common answer to a lot of questions around here."

The following month, while the children were being seen by Dr. Thomasson, I asked his nurse if she knew the answer to the mystery.

She just shrugged and replied, "That's the way it has always been."

I hid a small smile.

"Excuse me," a voice behind me said.

I turned around. An elderly lady in a green print dress motioned to me from a sofa in the waiting room.

"Come sit by me," she said, patting the seat beside her. "I'd be happy to tell you about those candles. I'm Grace Harding, and I live in the last house on the left. You know, the little red one?"

"Yes," I said. "I admired your beautiful bank of forsythia on the way into town."

"Forty years ago, when I married Henry and came to Snydersville, the first people to welcome us were the Johnsons, Clem and Anna. They had the farmhouse set back from the road."

I had seen the neat, white frame building set among its barns and outbuildings like a mother hen surrounded by her chicks.

"They had two sons, Arthur, the elder, a strong help-ful boy who took after his father, and James, a quiet sort. He liked to read books. He's a professor over at the state college now." She smiled at Sarah who was sitting beside me, listening intently.

"About a year after he'd left, the letters stopped coming. ... Then a man from the war office came by to tell them that Arthur was missing in action.

"When we began to have children, their daughter, Mary, used to mind them if we went to the cinema.

"Well, the war came along, and Arthur signed up. It nearly tore Anna apart, him being her firstborn and all. But he wouldn't be dissuaded. James stayed home and helped his father run the farm." She sighed. "A lot of the village boys went off to war."

Drawing herself back to her story, she continued, "Arthur wrote home regularly, and Anna used to read his letters to all the neighbors. She was very proud of him but worried, nonetheless. Mothers do that."

I nodded in agreement.

"About a year after he'd left, the letters stopped coming. Anna was just frantic. Then a man from the war office came by to tell them that Arthur was missing in action. They didn't know if he had been taken prisoner or ..." Her voice trailed off as she looked at Sarah, who was holding my hand tightly.

"That evening, Anna left the porch light on all night." ..."How long did she have to leave the porch light on?" I asked... "Until she died," she answered in a soft voice.

"That evening, Anna left the porch light on all night. Told Clem that she wouldn't turn it off until Arthur came home. A few days later I noticed that Ella Winter, down the road, had left her light on, too. So had the Moores. At twilight, I turned on a small lamp in my front window. It was the least I could do."

"How long did she have to leave the porch light on?" I asked, half dreading her response.

"Until she died," she answered in a soft voice. "After Arthur had been reported missing, I went to pay a visit.

When I turned to go, I noticed a big piece of tape over the switch to the porch light. Anna looked at it. 'No one touches that switch,' she said to me. 'Clem tried to turn it off one morning but I stopped him. Told him I didn't care about the electricity.' "

Mrs. Harding looked at Sarah and continued. "A few years later, those little electric Christmas candles came out, and the neighbors and I began burning them in our windows. We left them on for Arthur." She paused and then added, "And for all the others."

"The farmhouse still has its porch light on, doesn't it?" asked Sarah.

"Yes, dear," Mrs. Harding replied. "James lives in his parents' house now. The tape is still over the switch."

"Do you think Arthur might come back someday?" asked Sarah, her face full of worry.

"He might," Mrs. Harding said quietly.

"But he'd be very old, wouldn't he?" said Sarah.

"Yes, dear. He would be."

That evening after supper, I heard noises in the attic and felt the cool draft that always means someone has left the door at the top of the stairs open.

"Who's up there?" I called.

"Just me," Sarah's muffled voice responded.

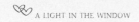

She came down the stairs with one of our window candles in her hand.

"I know it isn't Christmas yet, but I really want to put this in my window," she said, with a look that was at once hopeful and resolute.

"For Arthur?" I asked.

"Well, sort of," Sarah said. "But mostly for Kate. Maybe she's lost and just needs a light to guide her home."

I could not say no.

After I tucked her in, I stood in the doorway and looked at the candle.

Two weeks later, Kate returned followed by three kittens. Where she'd been, we'll never know. We were just glad to have her back.

"Can we leave the light on?" asked Sarah when we settled Kate into her basket. I nodded. For Arthur. And for all the others.

special occasions

Our friend Steve dropped by to borrow our truck last night and found us just finishing up dinner. My husband poured him a cup of coffee and he joined us at the table. Steve looked surprised as he sat down. "Do you have candles every night?" he asked. I nodded and smiled.

I remember that evening so long ago when I called the family to dinner only to have them stop in astonishment at the dining room door.

"Did I forget an important date?" asked Bob, warily eyeing the flowers and candles on the table.

"Is it somebody's birthday?" queried our son, Drew, as he sat down.

"Mommy, you look so pretty," Sarah said, noticing I'd exchanged my usual jeans for a dress. "Is somebody coming for dinner?"

"Well, " I began trying to put my feelings into words. "It's autumn, the air is crisp, the asters are coating the meadow with a frosting of purple, we're all healthy, and life is good."

The children gave each other their "Mom's-gone-round-the-bend-again" look and dug into their meatloaf.

That night, as I looked at my family around the table, I **realized** how much I take the future for granted. "Some day we'll..." is often heard at our house. But what if I knew just how many somedays were left to me? How would I live my life?

How could I explain to them my day spent helping my friend Linda? Linda's mother died three weeks ago. After the funeral, I'd offered to help her box up everything from her mother's house. I had done the same sad work a few years ago myself and knew how comforting it could be to have some company.

We started in the dining room. Linda sighed as she opened a drawer in the sideboard and pulled out a set of linen place mats and matching napkins, still in their original box.

"Mother bought these when she and Dad went to Ireland fifteen years ago," she said, running her fingers over the embroidery. "She never used them. Said they were for a special occasion."

When we opened the corner cupboard, Linda took down a set of crystal champagne flutes. "She never used these either," she said. "She bought them in Chicago and declared that we'd all get to toast Dad and her on their fiftieth anniversary. But Dad died shortly after their forty-eighth."

With her finger, she pinged the rim of one of the flutes, and we both listened to the clear tone. "They could have spent all those years drinking champagne together out of these lovely glasses instead of waiting for a day that would never be shared."

From her mother's closet upstairs, Linda pulled out a blue silk dress with rhinestone buttons. The price tag was still attached.

"Let me guess," I said. "For another special occasion?" Linda nodded sadly.

When I returned home that day, I caught up with some paperwork. My sister's birthday was in a few days, so I reached into the desk drawer where I keep greeting cards that I buy whenever I see a particularly appropriate one.

As I leafed through them, I came across one that said "For the World's Most Wonderful Mother." I never had a chance to send it to her, but I still cannot bring myself to throw it away.

That night, as I looked at my family around the table, I realized how much I take the future for granted. "Some day we'll..." is often heard at our house. But what if I knew just how many somedays were left to me? How would I live my life?

Well, for starters, I decided I'd clean house less and play with the children more. I'd read a book instead of finishing some project I thought was so important. I'd take more walks and more vacations, ride my bike and play the recorder. Polish my French instead of the silver.

I'd bear in mind that perfect is the enemy of good enough. I'd watch more sunrises (I'm not a morning person, but I can change) and try a new recipe every week (well, maybe twice a month). I'd call old friends and write to my sisters more often. I'd use perfume every day. And I'd always light candles at the dinner table.

My thoughts were interrupted by Eleanor asking, "Are you going to get dressed up every night now?"

"I just might," I replied.

"So can I wear my pink dress tomorrow night?" she asked, eyes wide with excitement.

I started to say that her pink dress was just for parties and church. I thought of all that extra ironing. Then I caught myself and answered, "Of course you can."

"I think we should make a toast," my husband declared, raising his water goblet. The children giggled and lifted their glasses of milk high.

"To life. To being together. To special occasions," Bob said, meeting my eyes knowingly.

"I'll drink to that," I said, clinking my glass with everyone's in turn. "May they happen often."

And they have.

"So can I wear my pink dress tomorrow night?" she asked, eyes wide with excitement. I started to say that her pink dress was just for parties and church. I thought of all that extra ironing. Then I caught myself and answered, "Of course you can."

a soaring of hawks

We've come to that time of year when the daytime haze no longer obscures the mountains and the evenings have a bit of a nip to them. Neighborhood children wear light jackets as they wait for the school bus in the cool of the early morning. The reds and golds of autumn have just begun to touch the treetops. Sweater weather, Mother used to call these early October days. At our house, these are all sure signs that the hawks will soon be here.

As if on cue, a dark speck appears on the horizon. My husband lifts the binoculars off their hook and goes out to the porch to scan the skyline. By the time I've found a sweater, two more specks have joined the first.

"Hawks?" I ask.

"Can't tell," Bob says, lowering the glasses for a moment. "Too far away. Might be turkey vultures." The dark forms and swirling flight patterns of vultures and raptors are similar; it is easy to mistake them from a distance.

Living in the foothills of the Blue Ridge Mountains, we are often treated to the sight of a hawk spiraling above our meadow. There is a quick flutter of wings as it hovers above its prey. Suddenly the hawk plunges toward the earth, wings tucked close to its body, looking as though it will surely crash. Then, at the last instant, it reaches out its talons, secures the catch, and swoops upward.

There is an old, dead tree in the lower field on which hawks like to perch. When it was first struck by lightning, we thought about taking it down, but now we would not dream of doing so. On the topmost branch of this old snag, the hawks sit, quietly surveying the meadow below with imperial hauteur, as though it were a grand buffet table set especially for them. We love to watch them soaring and then diving toward earth in what looks like a kamikaze mission. Sometimes, they succeed in catching their prey; other times, they don't.

It was at just this time of year, long ago, that our son, Drew, first spotted an announcement in the paper headlined Hawk Watch This Saturday. He read the details to us at the dinner table. "Come join the Nature Center at

the Inn on the Mountain and help us count the hawks as they migrate. Bring a lunch and chairs. Drinks provided."

The morning of our first hawk watch dawned clear and sunny. The girls helped me make peanut butter and jelly sandwiches; Drew and Bob found our beach chairs. We bundled the kids into the car and set off to the top of the Blue Ridge. There was no missing the Nature Center group. Off in the corner of the inn's parking lot, an assortment of trucks and cars were gathered. Children darted among the lawn chairs set out on the asphalt; a few were flying kites. Sunlight glinted off dozens of upraised binoculars.

We carefully threaded our way through the parked cars and found a spot near the edge of the lot where we could spread our blanket on the grass. When we opened the car doors, the children tumbled out excitedly and ran to join some friends. The joyous hubbub quickly subsided whenever someone shouted "There's one!" Heads turned upward; necks craned for a better view.

The afternoon wore on, but few hawks were spotted. The children were beginning to get restless. As we headed back to the car, a man from the Nature Center called out, "Sorry for the poor showing. It's early in the season yet. Come back next week." We waved a noncommittal goodbye and headed down the mountain.

It wasn't what we'd expected. Somehow, watching for hawks in the middle of a sea of asphalt, surrounded by cars and aluminum beach chairs, was not the quiet commune with Nature we'd hoped for. We all decided that we wanted to do this again but we needed to find a better spot, somewhere quieter and higher and closer to the hawks.

The following Saturday, the children were eager to be off to the "secret spot" that Bob had researched as ideal for hawk watching. We'd have to do some hiking, he said, so

> We love to watch them soaring and then diving toward earth in what looks like a kamikaze mission.

Drew whipped up a batch of our favorite trail mix. The girls made little pillows from my scrap basket, for they had decided the best way to watch for hawks was flat on their backs. We loaded everyone into the station wagon and headed for the mountains.

Our old car skittered on the loose gravel as we headed up the Gap Road. Two centuries ago, settlers' buckboards had made their way up this slope as they headed west over the Great Blue Wall, as the mountains were sometimes

called. If they could make it up this peak in covered wagons, we could certainly do it in a station wagon, I thought, as I looked nervously at the steep dirt road before us.

The spent seedpods of the mountain laurel stood out against the shiny green leaves. They grew tall as they struggled up beneath the towering oaks and sycamores in their search for sunlight. A small stream had escaped from its culvert and burbled across the road. The children cheered as we crossed it with a splash. The old road ended at a gate hung with a sign that told us we had reached the national park boundary.

We piled out of the car and, donning our backpacks, headed up the fire road toward the top of Pasture Mountain. A half hour later, the trees began to thin; those that remained were gnarled and twisted as they clung to the meager soil of the mountainside. At the top of the

"It's a kettle," Bob replied in a hushed tone, as though he feared the sound of speech might break the spell that seemed to bind the birds together. ... There must have been 100 or more hawks all circling together in a graceful dance.

mountain, Eleanor found a large patch of soft moss. We spread out our blanket and began unpacking our sandwiches.

"Look!" shouted Drew as he pointed overhead. High above us, circling lazily on a thermal of warm air was a hawk. Behind it, two more beat their wings to join him.

"Wow," sighed Eleanor. "Three at once." By the time we finished lunch, we'd counted seven more.

The northwest wind, moving across the Shenandoah Valley, hits the mountains and rises up in invisible spirals. Glider pilots love these thermals and so, obviously, do hawks. All afternoon, a steady stream of hawks flew overhead: sharp-shinned and Coopers, red-tailed and broad-wing. The girls handed out the pillows, and we lay on the soft moss and counted the hawks.

The warm, October sun soon lulled the children to sleep. The last thing I remember hearing before I, too, began to doze was Sarah's sleepy voice murmuring "Twenty-seven, twenty-eight . . ."

I woke with a start when Bob gently nudged me and whispered "Look." The children were already awake and gazing in awe as high above us five hawks circled slowly. Several more joined them, and soon there were more than two dozen hawks spiraling together, dark against the brilliant autumn sky.

"What is that, Dad?" Drew asked as he stared at the amazing black funnel of birds.

"It's a kettle," Bob replied in a hushed tone, as though he feared the sound of speech might break the spell that seemed to bind the birds together.

More birds streamed down from the north and joined the kettle until it seemed as though there must have been 100 or more hawks all circling together in a graceful dance. Then, slowly, a few broke away. Gradually, the dark funnel of hawks began to dissolve until just a few were left. And then, they too were gone.

Quietly, without our bidding, the children began to gather up their things. We hiked down the mountain in silence as though discussing what we had just seen might ruin the magic of the moment. As we left the windswept openness of the knob and entered the scraggly forest, Sarah began to spin. "Look, Mom," she shouted with delight. "I'm a hawk!" Eleanor joined her, and they swirled around each other, laughing. Drew followed at a more dignified pace.

Bob took my hand and smiled at our girls running and spinning down the trail. "I guess it won't be too long before they fly off on their own, will it?"

My heart ached at the thought. But I realized that this was what our job as parents was all about: to raise our children up to have the strength to soar off alone.

The touch of Bob's arm brings me back to the present. "Now that one is definitely a hawk," he says, pointing at a circling bird and handing me the binoculars. "This weekend, let's go up to the mountains." I nod in happy agreement.

We've continued to return to that same mountaintop each autumn; only now it is just the two of us. As we climb the trail, I always remember the magical day we saw the kettle; we've never seen another one. As Bob predicted, our children have, indeed, all flown off. But they come back often. And they have all soared.

Bob took my hand and smiled at our girls running and spinning down the trail. "I guess it won't be too long before they fly off on their own, will it?" My heart ached at the thought. But I realized that this was what our job as parents was all about. . .

angels, stars, and cowboy boots

The year our first child was born, I gave him a special Christmas tree ornament, a star of his very own. Over the years, I have given him ornaments that reminded me of him or marked an important milestone in his life. When his sisters arrived, they, too, received an ornament each year. Slowly, our family tree became laden with wonderful, one-of-a-kind decorations, rich with remembrance. As we gather each year to trim the tree, we unwrap these treasured ornaments, laughing and reminiscing about the meaning behind each little keepsake.

On the Christmas that our second child, Eleanor, was five, we had just had another daughter. That year, I found a wonderful angel holding the hand of a littler one. "This is you," I told Eleanor, "and the little one is Sarah, who is holding tight to your hand because you are going to be such a wonderful big sister."

Because the ornaments belonged to them, I have always allowed the children to unwrap their treasures and put them on the tree themselves, no matter how young they were. On occasion, these ornaments were used as toys and it shows. There is a feathered bird that is rather bald, a wooden train with no smokestack, and a felt gingerbread man whose buttons have disappeared. Things that are well loved often look that way.

Eleanor always laughs as she unwraps her little angels, who have been hung on the tree for twenty years, and remarks on a missing wing. "Was that an accident," she asks, "or a reflection on the fact that I have not always been angelic?"

She loves the crystal ballerina that I gave her the year she began ballet lessons. While the little dancer spins on her satin ribbon, Eleanor recalls the difficult choice she once had to make between becoming a professional ballerina or going to college. She chose the latter and has never regretted it. Her senior year in college, one of her roommates, spoofing Eleanor's dread of spiders, made her a special "spider swapper"—a flyswatter mounted on the end of a six-foot pole. To commemorate that joke, I gave Eleanor a carved Miss Muffet with a tiny spider sitting beside her.

Our youngest, Sarah, was very attached to her teddy bear. Needless to say, bears abound in her ornament box— carved, china, stuffed. A sparkling, golden bicycle marks the achievement of having learned to ride a two-wheeler and a replica of an antique plane commemorates her first airplane ride. For her fifth birthday, she was given a kit-ten; that Christmas, I found a little ornament with a fuzzy kitten curled up in a tiny straw basket.

Each year, as Sarah carefully unwraps her ornaments, she fondly remembers our many trips together: the week in San Francisco, where I found her the little wooden cable car, for instance, or the visit to Hawaii, marked by the straw palm tree.

The year she went on an Outward Bound sailing course, I gave her a little boat to celebrate her surviving her "solo" three days alone on a desert island. Last year, she remarked, "I'm not unwrapping ornaments, I'm unwrap-ping memories."

Drew, our firstborn and an enthusiastic athlete, has a stuffed–felt soccer player and a wooden skier, a china tennis racquet, and a carved kayak. As a child, his charging about the house earned him the nickname Drew the Dragon. So, of course, his box holds an intricately embroidered Chinese dragon, as well as a green ceramic one from Mexico.

As his interests turned to writing, I found Drew a wonderful Victorian scribe intently bent over a desk, a quill pen in his hand. When he was in college, he climbed Half Dome Mountain in Yosemite. To celebrate that conquest, I gave him a little hiking boot from Germany.

Several years ago, Drew married and moved out West. As our first Christmas without him approached, I climbed the winding staircase to the attic to look for the box of decorations. I paused to look out the tiny garret window at the fields beyond. Snow was beginning to cover the stub-

Slowly, our family tree became laden with wonderful, one-of-a-kind decorations, rich with remembrance. As we gather each year to trim the tree, we unwrap these treasured ornaments, laughing and reminiscing about the meaning behind each little keepsake.

ble of the autumn harvest. It was clear that we would be having a white Christmas. Behind a crate marked wreaths and next to the box containing the crèche, I found the carton marked "Children's Ornaments." I opened it.

Drew's box was easy to spot; he'd drawn a big dragon on the top when he was eight. Taking off the lid, I unwrapped a few ornaments: the skiing polar bear he got for his tenth Christmas, the Indian explorer I gave him the year he became a Boy Scout. Then, I came across my favorite, the little pair of miniature cowboy boots I gave him the year his father brought him back a real pair from Montana. Drew had refused to wear any other shoes for eight months.

As Sarah carefully unwraps her ornaments, she fondly remembers our many trips together ... "I'm not unwrapping ornaments, I'm unwrapping memories."

I rewrapped the little boots in tissue paper. Then, I carefully put everything back in the box and took it downstairs. In the warm kitchen, now fragrant with the armloads of evergreen boughs cut that morning, I wrapped up Drew's ornaments in brown paper and twine.

Long ago, when I gave my first baby his first ornament, I had decided that, when my children married and had homes of their own, I would give them their ornaments. It was time to send Drew his. The little box was the seed from which his own tree of ornaments would grow.

I walked into the village to post the package, imagining Drew's surprise upon receiving it. As snow fell on the path before me, I smiled at the thought of the pleasure he would have telling his wife about each ornament, its history, and its meaning.

Several Christmases ago, Drew's gift to us was the news that we would become grandparents in a few months' time. I realized with delight that there would be a new little person on my Christmas list; another generation of tree trimmers has begun.

A star was just the right first ornament for a first grandchild. Someday, when her father lifts her up to place it on the tree, he will tell her, "This is your very first ornament, given to you the year you were born." Then he'll point to his own little star twinkling on another branch and say, "And that one over there; that one was mine." Her eyes will grow wide with Christmas wonder. A tradition will continue.

the
christening
gown

Several months ago, our son, Drew, called. "Hi Mom," he said. "You're going to be a grandmother again."

Although I had been anticipating the news for some time, I was not prepared for the tears that suddenly filled my eyes. As I hung up the phone and told my husband the news, he grabbed me, and we danced around the kitchen, whooping with laughter. When we caught our breath, Bob said, "Looks like the christening gown will be worn again."

I nodded and looked back a few years to when our first grandchild, Carter Elisabeth, was born. The first thing I did when I learned of her impending arrival was to find the family christening gown. I had not seen it in nearly twenty-five years.

As I climbed the stairs to the attic, I remembered how carefully I had packed the gown away after the christening of our last baby. I had wondered then how many years would pass before I would get it out again.

I found the box lying in a dim corner. Carefully untying the ribbons that fastened the lid, I unfolded the tissue paper and caressed the soft, creamy folds of silk.

The gown is so old that its once-sparkling whiteness has softened to a pale ivory. The narrow hand-sewn seams are carefully rolled so that no rough stitching will ever touch a baby's soft skin. Delicate handmade lace edges the little collar and sleeves, and rows of little tucks have accommodated babies both large and small. The gown has been worn both by tiny newborns and strapping one-year-olds; it has been taken in and let out many times.

Five generations of Bedfords have worn this gown and its matching silk coat and bonnet. The initials of each child and his or her birthdate have been carefully embroidered in the lining—some more skillfully than others.

"I don't know how to embroider!" I confessed to my grandmother as my firstborn's christening day approached.

"Here, dear, I'll show you," she patiently replied as she set me to work practicing on a bit of muslin. The thread broke, knots formed, letters straggled.

"Won't you please do it?" I begged.

She simply shook her head. "It's a mother's privilege," she said.

After a week of practice, I finally felt up to the task and carefully embroidered W.A.B. 8-2-1964. Grandmother was proud of me.

As I lifted the dress and looked at my handiwork, I was, too. With each child, I'd grown more proficient. Drew's initials had been done in tiny cross-stitch; Eleanor's were in block; Sarah's flowed in curlicues. I ran my fingers up the long row of initials and dates until I reached the first set: N.P.B. 1-4-1863.

Packed into the box with the christening gown is a little pouch containing photographs of almost all the babies who have worn this dress. I unfolded the faded velvet case that holds the daguerreotype of the first baby to wear the gown. Nathan Peter rests in the arms of Grandmother Lovelace, looking very serious indeed. He was christened in Lauderdale County, Tennessee, on the eve of the Civil War. Grant marched near the Bedford farm later on but left the homestead untouched.

In the next picture I see Nathan Peter as a proud father. He is holding his infant son, Nathaniel Lynn, who pulls at the ribbons of the bonnet. Standing behind her husband is Katie Lynn Robert Bedford. In less than a year she would be a widow and return to the home of her father, a

As I climbed the stairs to the attic, I remembered how carefully I had packed the gown away after the christening of our last baby. I had wondered then how many years would pass before I would get it out again.

doctor, whose grandfather had fled France to help found the Huguenot Church in South Carolina. Little Nathaniel was raised by four widows: his mother, his grandmother, and two aunts—not an uncommon household for the post–Civil War South. No wonder he ran away from home at fourteen to become a cabin boy on a ship bound from Savannah. Twenty years later, however, he looks quite the respectable businessman as he poses with his son, Nathaniel Forrest, outside a church in Jacksonville, Florida. Little Nathaniel plays with the flower pinned to his father's lapel. Nathaniel's mother came to America from a tiny European country that has now disappeared from the maps. She did not believe in banks, preferring instead to invest in jewelry. One of her rings was given to me when I married her grandson.

My husband was the next baby to wear the christening dress. A Yankee by accident, he was born in Boston

when the Army sent his father there to attend radar school at M.I.T. during the Second World War. The little family was soon posted to Hobe Sound, Florida, so, as his Georgian grandfather was fond of saying, at least Bob was christened in the South. In the photograph, Bob is asleep in his mother's arms while his father, dressed in his captain's uniform, looks on proudly. After the war ended and Bob's father returned from the Pacific, the little family grew quickly. Bob soon had three sisters. Although they all wore the christening gown, not all of their pictures are in the envelope. As Bob's mother says, "When you have four children, some things get forgotten."

Five generations of Bedfords have worn this gown and its matching silk coat and bonnet. The initials of each child and his or her birthdate have been carefully embroidered in the lining—some more skillfully than others.

Our own children's christenings marked new chapters in our marriage, for each was born in a different city. The happy memories of every new home are captured in the photographs of our babies' christenings.

The christening gown has traveled with each generation, first by flatboat, later by horse and wagon, then by steamship, automobile, and truck. For Carter, it made its first trip by plane. The previous wearers had all been Eastern babies, but for Carter's christening, the little dress traveled to the mountains of Utah.

I carefully mended a seam and checked the stitching on the tiny pearl buttons, then I folded it gently back into its box. Smoothing the soft silk in place was like touching a butterfly's wing. It is delicate but enduring. Despite more than a century of christenings, the precious heirloom looks as though it could be worn for a century more.

As I walked to the village to mail the gown, I pondered my new role. For thirty years I had worn many hats: wife and mother, farmer and writer. I realized that I would soon have a new hat to wear—a grandmother's hat.

Carter had not even arrived yet, but already I felt venerable, as though a mantle of wisdom had been gently placed upon my shoulders.

At the post office, I met an old friend, Guy, who had been a grandfather for at least a dozen years. As we stood in line, I told him the good news of the soon-to-be birth of our first grandchild. I confessed to being a bit nervous in the new role and asked him what being a grandparent

truly means. "A grandparent," he told me solemnly, "is someone who tells the stories."

I told him . . . of the soon-to-be birth of our **first grandchild** . . . and asked him what being a grandparent truly means. "A grandparent," he told me solemnly, "is someone who tells the stories.

"Well then, here, Sonja," I said as I pushed my package across the counter to our postmistress clerk. "Send this off to Drew and Jill. It will be the first chapter of the old stories."

Soon the christening gown will be worn again by the latest addition to the newest generation. Sitting on the porch, sipping tea, Bob and I wonder out loud how many more times it will be worn by our grandchildren. Where else will it travel? Will we live to see it worn by our great-grandchildren?

I smile. The answers to those questions will be part of the new stories. I look forward to telling them.

the
golden
thimble

Henderson Baker's hay and feed store is nestled in a hollow in the Blue Ridge Mountains. Toward the back of the store, behind the feed sacks, is a dusty spot where people leave things for him to sell. That's where I first spotted the old sewing machine.

"When did you get this in, Henderson?" I called out from the dim corner.

"Sally Harris brought it by last month," he replied. "Said she found it in her uncle's barn up near Red Hill."

I love these old machines, especially their ornate, cast-iron bases. We put two of them together to make our breakfast table. Another serves as a nightstand, combined with a marble top I rescued from a drawerless bureau.

With old sewing machines the bases are usually the only part that is salvageable. The one in Henderson's store appeared to be no exception. The veneer was peeling and the drawers had been stripped of their brass pulls, but I knew that once the base was scraped, painted a glossy black, and topped with a piece of slate, it would make a perfect porch table. Henderson helped me load it onto my truck.

Back in my workshop, I lifted up the cover to the cabinet and had to catch my breath. Tucked away safely inside was the original machine. Its shiny black enamel and intricate gold ornamentation were in pristine condition. A wooden spool of thread was still in place. Its leather cable hung limply from the drive wheel. With a screwdriver, I slipped the belt back in place before adjusting the tension.

I lifted up the cover to the cabinet and had to catch my breath. Tucked away safely inside was the original machine.

Then I pulled up an old barrel, sat down, gingerly placed my foot on the treadle, and pressed down lightly. The machine still worked! A few drops of oil later, it began a contented whir as I pumped the treadle.

Looking for a scrap of fabric, I pried open one of the drawers. It contained a length of muslin, carefully wrapped around pieces of eyelet lace and blue ribbons. Beneath the muslin, a wooden darning egg nestled in some khaki-green socks whose heels still needed attention. A little pincushion, with a cross-stitched design of a ladybug on the top, bristled with needles and pins like a rusty porcupine.

I opened the other drawer, which held a half-knit child's sweater and, beneath it, a bundle of papers tied with red yarn. I carefully undid the little packet and spread out yellowed newspaper clippings, old letters, and faded photographs on my worktable. Among the pictures was a studio portrait of a handsome young man resplendent in a First World War uniform. A sepia photograph revealed a curly-haired toddler holding tightly to someone's leg. Another photo—taken a few years later—captured the child's dimpled smile and her dark curls caught up in a big bow. She was dressed in a white pinafore, edged in eyelet, and was pushing a china doll in a wicker baby carriage.

One newspaper clipping announced the marriage of Miss Adeline Booth to Mr. Emery Thackery on October 3, 1912. Another told of the departure of the Red Hill Guards to service in France in August of 1917. Several letters written to "Addie" by Emery described the beauty of France and the horrors of war. He closed

each letter with "be sure to kiss little Emmie for me."

Leafing through the papers, I came upon an invitation to an American Library Association meeting and two ticket stubs to The Nutcracker in Richmond. I also discovered a poem in childish handwriting and a first-grade report card dated June 6, 1920. A Miss Emma Thackery had earned A's in penmanship, reading, and geography, and B's in arithmetic and citizenship.

As I closed the bottom drawer, a sock got caught. I jerked it free, and a little red leather case flew out and landed on the floor. Carefully opening it, I discovered a small golden thimble with the letters E.W.T. to A.E.B. engraved around its base. It glittered in the palm of my hand.

The next morning, I went to the Historical Society on Court House Square to try to find the Thackery family. In the newspaper file, I learned that the Red Hill Guards had returned from France "much decorated, to a hero's welcome on the station platform" on January 23, 1919. Eleven names were listed as returning; Emery's was not among them.

Over at the courthouse, I found the records of Adeline and Emery's marriage and the birth of their daughter, Emma Marie. Emery was listed as a farmer. In the file of death certificates, one read: "Emery Wallace

Thackery, age 31, died at Côte de Chatillon, France, on October 16, 1918." The war ended less than a month later. The last Thackery to graduate from the high school had done so in 1931. A search of the current phonebook for Thackerys proved fruitless.

I sighed in frustration. Then I remembered the invitation to the Library Association's meeting and went home to write them to see if Adeline had ever been a member. Two months later, a pale blue envelope arrived in my mailbox from the association's secretary. She told me that Mrs. Emery Thackery had been a member of their society from 1911 until 1962 and had been the librarian at a private girls' school in Virginia's Tidewater.

... a little **red leather** case flew out and landed on the floor. Carefully opening it, I **discovered** a small golden thimble ...

I made a quick phone call to the school and explained my quest to the headmistress. Mrs. Thackery had been a much-beloved member of the school staff, the headmistress told me, but she had died in 1978. Hearing the disappointment in my voice, she told me that Adeline's

daughter was an alumna. Emma had married a Mr. Paul Hillman and lived in a town only eight miles from my home! I hung up the phone, smiling with satisfaction.

I looked up Mrs. Hillman's number and made another call. When I told her about the papers and the little thimble, she graciously invited me to her home for tea. A few days later, I pulled up at the Hillman home and knocked on the door. A young woman whose curly, dark hair and round face resembled the little girl in the faded photograph opened the front door.

"Hello," she smiled. "I'm Emily Lloyd; my grandmother is expecting you."

When I saw her, I knew at once that Mrs. Hillman had most certainly been the child in the photographs in the sewing machine cabinet. The curls were now silver, but her round cheeks still dimpled when she smiled. She took my hand and drew me down beside her on the sofa. I carefully spread out the little packet of papers and explained how I had found them.

"Mother cherished this and always kept it in her jewelry box. But when we moved, it vanished," she said. "It was Father's wedding gift to her."

Reaching for the photograph of the little girl in the pinafore, she said, "Here I am on my fifth birthday. My father sent me that doll from France." Then she touched the photograph of the soldier and said quietly, "And this was my father." Picking up the picture of the toddler she added, "This was me, and I think those are his legs for, you see,"—she pointed to the kneesocks—"those were part of his uniform. He left for the war when I was four and died in France."

I nodded, then asked, "Do you remember him, Mrs. Hillman?"

"Emma, please," she corrected me gently and continued, "Just little things, really. I can recall the sweet scent of his pipe and the feel of his tweed jacket against my cheek. He always kept peppermints in his pocket and let me find one there every evening after dinner."

I reached into my pocket and gently placed the red-leather case in Emma's hand. She opened it slowly and placed the thimble on her finger. It glimmered softly in the late afternoon light.

"Mother cherished this and always kept it in her jewelry box. But when we moved, it vanished," she said. "It was Father's wedding gift to her."

Emily brought in tea and admired the little thimble, as I told them how I had found the sewing machine. I

related my search for the sewing machine's owner, the piecing together of clues, the letters, and the phone calls.

"How well I recall that wonderful machine," Emma said wistfully. "I used to think it was magic; Mother could make anything on it. Anything! All I had to do was admire a dress in a store window, and she would make one just like it for me—better actually. My dolls had wardrobes fit for a queen."

She reached for a photograph. "I'm sure she made this pinafore. And that doll had a wardrobe that would make a princess jealous." She continued with a laugh, "How I loved playing beneath the machine and pushing the treadle up and down—even though I got scolded for doing so!"

"When did you last see it?" I asked.

"Well," Mrs. Hillman thought a moment, "after Father died, Mother tried running the farm with some help from her brother, but she just couldn't make a go of it. When the school offered her a job as a librarian and housemother complete with rooms for us and a scholarship for me, she sold the farm to our neighbor. Our quarters were so tiny, we just didn't have room for the sewing machine, and so she had to leave it behind."

"I can deliver it to you tomorrow," I said suddenly. "It works just fine."

"No, no," Emma said, shaking her head. "I wouldn't hear of such a thing. The thimble and photographs are enough."

"But you must take it," I said. "It really doesn't belong to me. When I think of the special occasions it was used for, the lovely things it created, I cannot keep it. The memories are yours, not mine."

She hesitated. "Besides," I concluded, "I only wanted the base, not the machine. I can always find another."

"Thank you," Emma said softly. "That would be lovely." Then she smiled and said, "Emily is getting married this fall." Turning to her granddaughter, she asked, "Wouldn't it be wonderful if we could make your wedding dress on Mother's old sewing machine?"

Emily hugged her grandmother with delight. Then she poured us a second cup of tea and begged Emma to tell

Turning to her **granddaughter**, she asked, "Wouldn't it be wonderful if we could make your **wedding dress** on Mother's old sewing machine?"

her more about her great-grandmother. As rain pattered gently against the windows, we listened to Emma's tales of her mother and of her tireless effort to run a farm—she, a city girl from Richmond. Emma told us of her mother's love of books and her determination to be a librarian in an age when women didn't usually have careers.

And she spoke of her mother's patience in teaching her the art of sewing. "A precious gift," she reflected. "One I have always treasured."

A few weeks ago, Emily and her fiancé came to fetch the sewing machine. Yesterday, the postman arrived at my door with a small parcel. I opened it to find a beautiful quilted tea cozy and matching napkins with hand-crocheted edges. The little note that was tucked in the box read, simply, "Thank you. From Emma (and Adeline)."

a walk
with a
child

My granddaughter, Carter, and I are going for a hike. I've loaded my pack with some crackers and some grapes, lemonade, and a diaper.

When Carter's father was a boy, we took many family hikes—through the rain forests of Washington's Olympic peninsula, up the White Mountains of New Hampshire, among the valleys of the Blue Ridge Mountains. The family photo albums are full of pictures of Drew and his sisters carving special walking sticks, posing in the gnarled roots of gigantic trees, or terrifying me by hanging over sheer cliffs. But it's been a long time since I took a hike with a two-year-old.

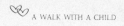

I figure, in an afternoon, we can go a mile or two, perhaps from Carter's house to the first meadow and back. The trails here in the mountains of Utah can be steep. I know that on the way home, I may have to carry her piggyback for a bit. This thought makes me extra glad that Drew and Jill did not wait any longer to have children. Were I ten or fifteen years older, hoisting a grandchild up on my back might be out of the question.

Carter leads the way with a **little step** that makes her look like a frisky colt, sort of a **cross** between a gallop and a skip. "Good," I think. "This is a fine pace. We'll make **good time**."

As we near the trail, my eyes take in the lovely woods, the colorful wildflowers, the dramatic rock outcroppings. But we've a hike to do, so I don't dally. Carter leads the way with a little step that makes her look like a frisky colt, sort of a cross between a gallop and a skip.

"Good," I think. "This is a fine pace. We'll make good time."

Suddenly Carter hunkers down in the trail. "A stick, Gammy," she says, picking it up. She discovers another one and declares, "Two sticks." She places them in my hand for my inspection.

"Very pretty," I say, taking the little sticks and putting them in my pocket. Then I take her hand and lead her onward. "Here we go."

We walk hand in hand for two or three minutes until a flash of red catches Carter's eye. "Ooooo, pretty," she says and darts off the trail. Caught in the light of a sunbeam, a bright-red clump of cardinal flowers glows in the shadows of the forest. I follow and find her stroking the delicate blossoms. She looks up at me tentatively.

"Pick it?" she asks.

"Just one," I say. "We want to leave some for other people to see."

Carter solemnly picks one tiny bloom and lays it gently in my hand. "Is booful," she says, and I nod in agreement. I put it in my pocket with the sticks.

A few hundred feet further we come upon a pile of boulders that had fallen from the cliffs high above. Of course they must be climbed.

As I hover behind Carter, hands ready to catch her, my mind drifts back thirty years as I remember watching her father climb the jungle gyms in New York's Central Park. Our first apartment was in an old brownstone on the East Side. The walk to the park was lined with brick stoops.

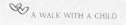

Drew knew every one of them; they were his Himalayas. Each low wall had to be climbed. Every phone booth became a playhouse. Fruit stands needed investigating (and an apple was invariably bought). Stoplights were carefully watched for the green. "OK, Mommy. Go!" Drew would shout as he galloped across the intersection, pulling me behind him.

A rock teeters beneath Carter's foot and I dart to catch her, but she regains her balance and climbs higher. The rhythm of living with little people seeps slowly back into my consciousness. Trust in their abilities. Bumps and falls teach them lessons my warnings never can. It's coming back to me now.

Drew moved to Utah so that he could ski steep slopes and climb tall mountains. Clearly, Carter is following in his footsteps. When she has carefully climbed down, we sit on a rock and share the crackers and lemonade. She gathers a few of the smaller stones and asks, "Pudit inna pocket?" I gladly oblige.

As we continue our hike (walk? amble?) I remember, too, that a walk with a child is about process, not completion. The goal of the meadow was mine, not Carter's. I slow down and let her set the pace.

By the side of the trail she spots a butterfly. I had not seen it. When you are less than three feet from the ground, you notice a great deal that we taller folk do not. The butterfly is dead, its bright markings dulled, its wings tattered. Carter holds it tenderly in her hand and strokes its furry body. Together we marvel at the colors of its wings. She throws it up in the air and orders, "Fly." But it drifts slowly back to earth. She carefully picks it up and gives it to me. It joins the other treasures in my pocket. I am beginning to feel like a walking Museum of Natural History.

A bit farther on, we see a line of ants marching across the trail. Carter is fascinated and flops down on the moist earth to inspect them. I hesitate, then realize that our clothes are washable and so are we. I lie down beside her. From this vantage point, the ants take on a whole new identity. They are not just tiny black spots but earnest workers on a mission. They pass one other, antennae waving, each one locked into her special job. Not for them a side trip to smell a flower or explore a hollow log.

"Ooooo, pretty," she says and darts off the trail. Caught in the light of a sunbeam, a bright-red clump of cardinal flowers glows in the shadows of the forest. I follow and find her stroking the delicate blossoms.

I place a twig in the ants' path to see what they will do. Without missing a beat, they climb right over it. Carter follows my lead and places a tiny pebble in a small break in the stream of ants. They climb over that, too. We add ever-bigger pebbles until finally we place one that is too large for the ants to climb. Their purposeful parade divides and flows around it. I tell Carter how they lay down a scent trail so they can find their way home and that, when they wiggle their antennae, it's like talking. How much of this she understands I don't know, but she lies quietly and listens as she watches the ants intently.

To walk with a **child**, I have remembered, is not about "getting there." It is about discoveries . . . and **rediscoveries**. "Thank you, Carter," I say softly.

Carter sits up slowly and rubs her eyes. "Go home now?" she asks. "See Mommy?" Ah, yes, I remember. When one is sleepy, home is best.

For the past few months, when someone asked her, "How old are you?" Carter has been replying, "I pushin' two." Tomorrow is her birthday; we are visiting for the festivities. Part of my reason for this outing with Carter is so that Jill can put up decorations and bake the birthday cake.

We start back down the trail, more slowly this time. We never did get to the meadow. As a matter of fact, we've probably gone no more than half a mile. But my pockets are bulging, and we've seen many new things.

I make a mental note that, next time, I shall tuck into my pack a magnifying glass and a small cushion for me to sit on while Carter digs holes in the dirt with a stick.

Carter begins to fret, so I move my pack around to the front and swing her up on my back. A tired little head bobbles against my shoulder. As I slow my pace, I notice a lovely patch of light green lichen with frilly edges. It looks like a celadon pillow edged in crochet. In my usual power-walk mode, I might have missed it.

To walk with a child, I have remembered, is not about "getting there." It is about discoveries ...and rediscoveries.

"Thank you, Carter," I say softly.

"Tankooo" echoes a sleepy, little voice.

The shadows lengthen on the path. In the distance, I can see Carter's house. Birthday balloons are already bobbing brightly on the mailbox. Jill has put her afternoon to good use. Then again, so have I.

a first
time for
fireflies

In the gathering twilight, furtive figures dart across the lawn. The song of the peepers and the katydids is accompanied by excited shouts of "Got one!" or "Quick, Daddy, catch it."

Our granddaughter, Carter, has discovered fireflies. In my own naïveté, I thought everyone knew what a firefly was. I was sure that, come summer, each and every town in America was decorated by the twinkling of their nighttime flights. But I was wrong.

On the first evening of their annual visit to our home in Virginia's Piedmont, we were sitting on the porch, lingering at the table after dinner, when suddenly Carter gasped, "Oh look, a shooting star!" Then, gazing about in confusion, she said, "And another one. And another."

We looked where she was pointing and saw the fireflies blinking their Morse code of love. In an instant, Carter was out of her chair, chasing the twinkling bugs and squealing in delight. Her little sister, Mason, sitting in her mother's lap, clapped her dimpled hands and cooed with pleasure. Our son, Drew, ran to join his daughter, saying, "I'd forgotten about the fireflies."

I turned to my daughter-in-law, who was smiling at the excitement of her family. "You don't have fireflies in Utah?" Jill shook her head. Of course not, I realized. Fireflies spend the day in the cool, damp grass. Then, when darkness begins to fall, they emerge into the coolness of evening and begin their courtship dance. Slowly, they rise to the tops of the trees, where they garland the branches like tiny ropes of twinkling diamonds. Utah is mostly desert. It is hot and dry, and there is no cool, deep grass for the fireflies.

During her visit with us, Carter has been busy discovering all the differences between our home and hers. "Let's walk down the hill to the pond," I suggested to Carter on the first day of her visit. She looked up at me, perplexed, and said, "This isn't a hill, Gammy!"

I laughed, as I realized that the gently rolling landscape of the Blue Ridge Piedmont is a far cry from the majestic Wasatch Mountains that surround her home in Utah. Accustomed to walking up her steep driveway, she ran right up our sloping one in thirty seconds flat, leaving me, the lowlander, puffing far behind. Everything here is new and different. Carter and Mason do not have Canada geese that honk loudly as they come in for a landing on the pond or a white horse who, with his two donkey friends, pokes his head over the fence, looking for handouts of carrots and apples. And they don't have fireflies.

Why is that that which we know, that which we have lived, we think to be the province of all people? When I went away to school, I was astonished that everyone there did not know how to sew. That was just part of growing up, I thought. Everyone learned how to sew. But most of my classmates had not. My surprise gave way to pleasure as I quickly discovered that I could earn spending money by mending and altering things for the other women in my dorm. I even began a small business making the A-line jumpers that were all the rage when combined with black tights and a turtleneck.

Over the years, I have discovered that assumptions can get me into trouble. I try to remember not to express surprise when others' lives and experiences do not match my

own. I do not always succeed. In my enthusiasm for learning more about other people and different cultures, I
sometimes rush pell-mell into conversations, without think-
ing. I'm working on that. So is our youngest daughter.

"You've never seen snow?" Sarah asked incredulously of
her fellow teachers, her first week at a boarding school in
Mobile, Alabama. Several shook their heads no.

> In my own naïveté, I thought everyone
> knew what a firefly was. I was sure that,
> come summer, each and every town
> in America was decorated by the
> twinkling of their night-time flights.

"Astonishing," she murmured, as they helped each
other move into the faculty apartments. "Well," one young
woman said, her arms full of books, "It did snow a little
bit when I was a kid. But I was asleep, and it was gone
before I woke up."

Two years later, when Sarah moved to New York, her
friend Scott offered to help her drive her U-Haul. "Maybe
I'll get to see snow," he said, hopefully. Their plan was to
make their first stop at our house. The night they arrived,
it was sleeting heavily. The driveway was a sheet of ice.

They got a running start and made it up the hill, then collapsed in exhaustion after sixteen hours of driving. When Scott awoke around noon the next day, five inches of fresh snow covered the ground with its soft whiteness. More was falling.

Sarah was ecstatic. "Do we still have a sled?" she asked eagerly. Of course we had a sled. No one gives away a sled. You never know when you might need one.

What fun it was to watch those two squeeze themselves onto a tiny red toboggan and careen down the hill. "Remember to bail out at the bottom," I called after them. "The pond's not frozen yet."

They sledded for half an hour, then made snow angels. A snowball fight and snowmen-making ensued. Looking out the frosted windows, I saw Scott catching snowflakes on his tongue. Just as my children had done, just as I had done before them. He was as excited as—well, as excited as Carter chasing her first fireflies.

What a pleasure it is to see someone experience a first joy or a new discovery. When our daughter Eleanor was a senior in high school, she spent the academic year in a little French village near Lyons. She wrote home of finally conquering the language, making friends, learning how to make cookies called langue de chat. Our Christmas present to her that year was an airplane ticket for her French "sister," Véronique, to come and visit us that summer. Véro had never been out of the Loire Valley.

"Quelle gros voiture," she said in amazement, when we picked her up at the airport in our ordinary, American sedan. It was billed as a midsize car, but it looked huge to her. And then we all laughed, Véro included, as her eyes grew big as saucers when a stretch limo drove by.

For a month, we saw our country through French eyes. Véro loved American food (although Eleanor was, by now, looking down her nose at it), thought having a little sister was chouette, and that hot dogs were equally cool. She was astonished by the size of our supermarkets and wished our American movies had French subtitles.

As a hostess present, Véro had brought us a tin of dried chanterelles that she and her parents had gathered in the woods of the Haute Loire. She showed me how to make potage aux champignons with them. I'd never made anything with dried mushrooms before, soup included, which surprised her, too. Now, her version of mushroom soup is one of my favorite recipes.

This evening, as I watch Drew show his daughter how to gently cup her hands around the glimmering fireflies, I reflect on the sense of wonder that children have, that we all have, actually, when confronted with something new and wonderful.

Tomorrow, Carter will have her very first ride on a pony. Our neighbor has a gentle brown mare named Montana, who, he says, can't wait to have a little girl on her back. I must look and see if I still have that old cowboy hat that Drew loved to wear when he was about Carter's age.

Drew races to the porch. "Have you got a bug jar, Mom?" he asks.

I know why he wants it. He and Carter will put a few fireflies in the jar and add some grass and a stick for climbing. And maybe, as he and his sisters used to do, they will add a little bottle cap full of water, in case the fireflies get thirsty in the middle of the night. The jar will rest by Carter's bed, and she will slowly slip off to sleep, watching Nature's nightlight softly glowing on the bedside table.

I know I've got a jar in the back of the cupboard somewhere—a peanut butter jar with lots of holes poked in the lid.

"Mom?" Drew asks again, bringing me back to the present.

"Of course, I have a jar," I laugh. "You never throw away a bug jar; you never know when you might need it."

He smiles, and suddenly I am not looking at my six-foot-three son but his three-foot-six former self who asked that same question so many years ago. First-time discoveries are wonderful. Second-time rediscoveries are pretty good, too.

migrations

It is unusually warm for March. The window in my study is open and soft breezes blow the curtains. Suddenly, I hear a distant noise; the sound is unmistakable. Geese. As the faint honking grows cacophonous, I look out the window above my desk and search the patch of sky above our woods. I know I will soon see the graceful birds as they make their approach, gliding in for a landing on the pond at the bottom of the hill. They are heading home.

In a slightly ragged V, fifteen geese drift across the pale, spring sky. I've been expecting them. The sound of their honking always stirs something in me, a longing, a yearning for my own ancestral home, miles to the north.

As I turn back to work, my eye falls on the large glass lamp casting a pool of yellow light on my desk. For as long as I can remember, I've returned from my grandparents' home on Cape Cod each summer with a small bit of the seashore: a chunk of sea glass, a shell, a small piece of driftwood. My lamp is filled with these treasures.

The paperweight that attempts to keep my pile of manuscripts orderly is a large whelk shell.

I put the shell to my ear and listen to whispering waves breaking on the sand. The summer I found it thrown high against the dunes by a winter storm I was about ten, the age when children begin to change from merely observing Nature to longing to know more about it. When we returned from the beach, I ran to show my grandmother my new treasure. She was where I knew she would be, in the garden behind her rambling old house. From its high terrace, she could look out across the tidal river, which nourished the life of the marsh. She had recently begun to show me the complex community of watery life that dwelled in the shadows of the dock and among the stiff marsh grasses—a community, she told me, that depended upon the ebb and flow of the tides.

In a slightly ragged V, fifteen geese drift across the pale, spring sky. I've been expecting them. The sound of their honking always stirs something in me, a longing, a yearning for my own ancestral home, miles to the north.

In her lap she had her ever-present binoculars, the ones she used to watch the birds that darted among high branches of the linden tree, or sipped nectar from her flowers. That summer she taught me the birds' names and how to distinguish their calls; she spoke of their long winter flights and how they returned each spring to their summer home—just as I did.

When I showed her my shell and told her I had heard the ocean in it, she smiled and said that, in a way, I was right. But, she explained, it was the ocean inside me that I heard, the essence of my life in the world, the exaggerated throbbing of my own heart, the whispering of my blood. The shell might have come from a long way off, she said. When I had asked if it might have come from as far away as the birds flew for the winter, she nodded.

Perhaps it was those summers by the river, on the marsh, along the shore, that helped form my belief that a woman's life is like the seasons. We reflect the slow cadence of nature's cycles. In our ability to create life and then nourish that life, we are like the sea itself from whose waters this world of ours once emerged. The sound we hear in a seashell is the same sound our children hear during the long months before their birth.

Each spring, as I watch the sky above my home fill with birds returning from their winter havens, I feel the pull of the shore. The rhythm of the season quickens. I become part of the migration and, like the generations before me, begin making plans for my summer by the sea.

Each spring, as I watch the sky above my home fill with birds returning from their winter havens, I feel the pull of the shore. . . . For all of us, no matter . . . how far away we have lived from family, these places are part of our roots. They nourish our souls.

I am not alone. Many of my friends speak of a special place that they, too, think of as their spiritual home. It may be a cabin by a lake, a little motel by the seashore, a campsite by a rushing stream, a lodge in a national park. It may be a house that has been in their family for generations, or just a spot to which they always return, every year or as often as they can. For all of us, no matter how often we have moved, how far away we have lived from family, these places are part of our roots. They nourish our souls.

Now I have grandchildren of my own. Like my own children, they will hear the stories of the past, learn about the life of the sea, and the birds, and the land. In them, the cycle of life begins anew.

Through the open window, I can hear the contented noises of the geese settling in for the evening. As I begin writing letters to my children, inviting them to our own annual migration, my gaze falls upon my shell. Perhaps, this summer one of my granddaughters will find a shell like mine. And, when she holds it to her ear, she will hear the sound that has always drawn me back to the shore. The sound of the sea and of summer and of the secret sounds deep within herself.

index